WASHINGTON

WASHINGTON

PHOTOGRAPHY

BY

RAY ATKESON

TEXT BY

CARL GOHS

Washington at Random

CONTENTS

Library of Congress Card Catalog Number 70-81401

Copyright© 1969 by

Publisher · Charles H. Belding

Designer · Robert Reynolds

Printer · Graphic Arts Center

Binder · Lincoln and Allen

Printed in the United States of America

First Printing

Right: Early morning at Cooper Lake in the Central Cascades east of Snoqualmie Pass in Wenatchee National Forest. The area is accessible from a Forest Service road that is an extension of State Highway 903 out of Cle Elum on the east slopes of the Cascades. The lake outlet is a tributary of the Cle Elum River.

Below: The late afternoon sun sidelights the rich rolling grain lands of the Palouse country in Southeastern Washington. The photograph was taken from summit of Steptoe Butte, a state park near U. S. Highway 195, between towns of Colfax and Rosalia.

Right: Sunlight, with difficulty, penetrates the dense upper story of foliage in the Rain Forests of Olympic National Park in the far northwest corner of Washington. Huge, contorted big-leaf maples, draped with moss, compete for space and light with fir, spruce, hemlock and cedar in the dark forests along the Hoh, Queets and Quinault rivers on west-slope Olympics.

Below: Sunlit waters of Buck Creek rush past a moss-covered boulder in the North Cascade Mountains. Countless similar streams race down from the steep, upper slopes from permanent glaciers or from great snowfields that blanket the heights most of the year.

Right: Bright sunlight reflects on Pacific breakers along the North Coast of Washington. A storm far at sea has churned the waters into foam that currents and winds have then cast up on the black sands.

Below: A pool near timberline in the Goat Rocks Wilderness, south of Mount Rainier in the South-central Cascades. The reflected trees are subalpine fir and mountain hemlock. Often, winds contort the trees into strange shapes such as that of the long-fallen, weather-bleached log at the edge of the pool.

Right: A part of a great flock of Canada geese migrating along Washington's Pacific Flyway at sunset.

Below: Backwash from one great, Pacific breaker meets headon with a second breaker to explode above a submerged rock near the edge of the shore.

Introduction

In the early 1800s, the Far West and the Northwest were an Ultima Thule—land as remote as Afghanistan or Tibet. If the West was more real to an Easterner, it probably was because it was a part of the same continent, although the opposite, outer edge. The State of Washington is the upper corner of that outer edge of the conterminous United States (the old forty-eight, before Alaska and Hawaii). The Columbia River forms about three-fourths of the southern boundary; the Pacific Ocean forms the west; Canada forms the north. The area that now is Washington very nearly remained British property. The dispute about the territory was the last Anglo-American border conflict in North America that came near to a real, fighting war.

After the American Revolution, England and the United States commenced almost a century of contention about the location of the Canada-United States boundary. In the West, English claims north of the Columbia River were especially strong. An Englishman was the first to sail and map Puget Sound; Canadian and English fur traders established the first posts east of the Cascades; the Hudson's Bay Company founded the first two major settlements in the Northwest—one on the north bank of the Lower Columbia, the other near the south end of Puget Sound. These were no mere outposts, but were developed into great estates, with fortifications, villages, farms and herds of cattle. Resident British subjects outnumbered American citizens about a hundred to one. Americans had two important prior claims: an American expedition was the first to pass the Rocky Mountains and enter the Columbia Basin, and an American seaman was the first to sail into the Columbia River. There matters stood. Both countries were nettled about the inconclusive War of 1812, and yet both tended to rattle sabers to reinforce an argument. The finale was comic, with echoes of laughter and a squeal.

About mid-century both British and American politicians ceased for a moment to play political games and agreed that the undecided western Canada-United States boundary should follow the forty-ninth parallel. On reaching Puget Sound, the boundary was to dip south a bit around Vancouver Island, thence run west through Juan de Fuca Strait to the Pacific. The treaty,

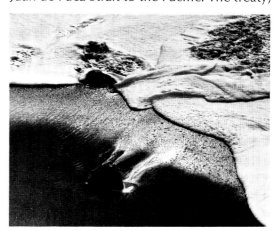

otherwise workable, neglected to account for the San Juan Islands. The San Juans are a delightful archipelago of a hundred and seventy-some islands scattered between the American mainland and Vancouver Island. The treaty language could be read two ways —one giving the San Juans to the United States, the other giving them to Canada. A decade passed. Families drifted to the larger islands, cleared land, and planted crops. Anglo-American jurisdictional disputes were inevitable. The confiscation (theft, the

English called it) by an American tax collector of some sheep belonging to English settlers that refused to pay an American land tax upset local government officials on both sides, but it went no further. Presumably, and understandably, friction remained. Finally, on big San Juan Island, an American's property was raided. An English pig invaded a neighboring American potato patch. Snorting and rooting, he triumphantly gobbled precious American potatoes. The American potato grower asked that the animal be penned. The English owner refused. Sorties into the potato patch continued until, one day, the American shot and killed the pig. Word of this reached the highest government levels in England and in the United States. American and British troups arrived, setting up camp at opposite ends of the island. The men of the opposing forces mixed congenially, however, and despite fifteen miles between camps, the men moved back and forth to exchange entertainments. Eventually, the English and American governments agreed to submit the argument to the German emperor for arbitration. He gave the San Juan Islands to the United States, and Washington's boundaries were secure and fixed at last.

The boundaries enclose sixty-eight thousand square miles. A view from about fifty miles aloft would reveal a generally rectangular shape measuring about three hundred miles east to west, by about two hundred miles north to south. The upper left corner is cut out, and into that space the lower end of Canada's Vancouver Island projects. The western third of the rectangle is virtually uniform green at any season. The eastern two-thirds, in early summer for instance, alternates from checkered patterns of the green of irrigated farms to broad, irregular patches of ochre and umber that are desert or semi-desert. The Cascade Mountains separate west from east, rising in a great wall of sharp peaks and ridges from Canada to the Columbia River.

The Pacific Coast of Washington has two large bays—Grays Harbor, and Willapa Bay — that between them occupy the greater share of the south. In the north, the Pacific cuts into the continent for about a hundred miles through Juan de Fuca Strait, then floods south creating the vast inland sea called Puget Sound. The Sound is many-armed and multiple-fingered. Very nearly a million acres of the state are inland waters, of which the Sound is the largest share. As the waters of Puget Sound mark Northwestern Washington, so water, in a sense, marks all of the state, either by its absence, or by its presence in many forms and guises. The Olympic and Cascade Mountains shine with water bound as snow and ice in more than a hundred living glaciers; Pacific headlands recede and disappear as winter fogs curl around their flanks and summits; rivers spin turbines by the dozens; flumes and ditches carry sparkling water to land with crops that otherwise would die; the Columbia, greatest river entering the Pacific anywhere, traces a long and meandering path across the state.

The Columbia rises in the Columbia Ice Fields high in the Canadian Rockies. It flows north for more than a hundred miles into British Columbia's interior, describes a wide arc, then turns south toward the northeast corner of Washington. The Columbia drains all of the state east of the Cascades, and large portions of neighboring states and British Columbia. It was in legend, and is in fact, the Great River of the West. Most of the Columbia's path is through a gorge varying from a mile or two wide, to more than a thousand feet deep. The gorge is often a hard edge against the land, a sharp lip, or rimrock, falling abruptly to the river's sides. Its passage through the Cascade Mountains is a succession of cliffs and pinnacles cut from black basalt, the spectacular evidence of a battle between water and buckling earth. Geologists say that the Columbia cut its channel at or near the rate that the Cascades rose. As the earth's crust split, belched lava, buckled and arched, the great river sought first one and then another course, following weaknesses in the surface. The channel one sees today is anything but straight. In Washington, although it flows generally south, and then west, it often does the opposite, and more than one motorist, crossing the state, has been astonished at finding himself following or crossing an *east* or *north* flowing river.

The Columbia's shifting course crosses two strikingly different landscapes. East of the Cascades the land is dry, and that to the west is moist. Annual precipitation, west, will mostly vary between thirty and forty inches; temperatures are mild; summers of prolonged ninety-degree days are rare, as are winters of prolonged subfreezing. East of the Cascades annual precipitation is more likely to vary between ten and about twenty-five inches; summer daytime temperatures are usually in the high eighties or middle nineties. In winter, snow is common, although prolonged sub-zero temperatures are uncommon. The forests are an infallible clue to climate—dense and dark in the west, light and open in the east. The forests, or at least their utilization and handling, also trace development of the state, from territorial days up to the present.

The first industry in the Pacific Northwest was a sawmill built by Hudson's Bay Company in 1827 in what now is Southwest Washington. It was a crude affair, and was followed by others, some ingeniously contrived, as settlers of the 1840s arrived. West of the Cascades, at that time, a man cleared a space on his land for a house, and in doing so, produced the materials with which to build his house. Trees grew as plentifully as prairie grass.

Ships and wagons brought men to the West in ever greater numbers; camps became towns and towns became cities — cities built of wood and brick, but mostly wood. Some cities burnt almost as fast as they were built. Discoveries of gold and silver in the West, and offers by the federal government of free land turned an orderly migration into a general exodus. The rapidly increasing population of the West drove lumber demands, and prices, to ever higher levels. Men came by ship with machinery for steam-power mills, and the first industry in the Northwest became *the* industry. It would remain so for a hundred years. From the simple beginnings near Fort Vancouver, lumbering shifted north to Puget Sound. The shift to the Sound, essentially, was unrelated to the northward population drift in Western Washington. The new towns and cities *were* markets, certainly, but the Puget Sound lumber industry would have been born, and would have flourished, independent of the local market. The reason was, that in terms of the technology of the day, the region was tailored to lumbering as was no other in all of the Pacific Northwest.

Three circumstances contributed: timber, terrain and transportation. The timber was a product of the climate. Lush forests grew easily; trees grew to great dimensions.

Trunks, six feet above flaring bases, measured six feet through. Sitka spruce and Douglas fir reached heights comparable to that of fifteen and twenty story buildings. The great trees seemed to number in millions. They grew to the water's edge along hundreds of miles of shore. The land surrounding much of the Sound is hilly, sometimes even mountainous. Hills slope to the edge of the water and often immediately plunge to depths that can easily accommodate ocean-going vessels. The steep terrain facilitated moving huge logs to water side. As early as the 1850s and 60s small steam tugs pulled rafts of logs to mills. On land, transportation was far more primitive. Oxen that had hauled settler's wagons across the plains went to work in the woods.

Roads were paths cleared downhill to mills or to log dumps on bays. Trees were cut into thirty or forty foot lengths for easier handling, and were skidded along primitive tracks. The track, or skid road, was made of transverse logs felled across a cleared path at intervals of about ten feet. Fish oil or some other lubricant greased the skids. Skid road became Main Street in the woods and in lumber camps and towns. *Skid Road* in time, entered the vocabulary to mean a street or district of tumble-down houses and cheap saloons. Terrain and skid roads helped get logs to mills or water, but equally important was shipping the lumber to market. Puget Sound's many bays and inlets formed a quiet waterway to the Pacific, in effect becoming a launching platform to world markets. Lumber schooners from New York and Boston called at mills on deep bays where hulls were filled with the sweet-smelling lumber. Further developments of steam power and of railroads pushed logging back into the hills beyond the mile or so that was the economic limit of skid roads. Mills were established at Grays Harbor on the Pacific, on the Strait of Juan de Fuca, and on the Lower Columbia. Completion of the transcontinental railroad opened all of the state to full-scale lumbering for United States and foreign markets.

More than half of the land area of Washington is classified as commercial forest land. About half of that is privately owned; the balance is divided among several federal or state agencies, chief of which are the

U. S. Forest Service and the Washington State Department of Natural Resources. The various public agencies establish annual cutting quotas, selling the standing timber by sealed bid to private companies. Quotas are calculated on a sustained yield that in theory balances annual cut with annual maturation. Many private timber owners follow similar cutting schemes.

The Northwest forests were a mixed blessing to the first settlers, impeding men and wagons. Especially was this true west of the Cascades. Huge trees grew on most of that land suitable for food crops, so men cut trees (and often burned whole tracts) and

blew up or burned the stumps (sometimes the size of a cabin). The products of the first land farmed were for home consumption; later, as more land was cleared, farmers traded with townsmen for needed goods. Wagons carted wheat and wool to rivers to be barged downstream to ports for transshipment or for local milling. Rivers and waterways that served logging and lumbering served the farmer as well. A rich fisheries developed on the Lower Columbia, Willapa Bay, Grays Harbor and Puget Sound. The superb king, tyee or Chinook salmon, and silver salmon, were packed in barrels or in tins and shipped to distant markets. Pacific Bays and the Sound gave up clams and oysters in magnificent abundance. Land was found in Eastern Washington that produced wheat in almost unbelievable yields per acre; and wherever water was available for irrigation, orchards produced apples, cherries, peaches and pears.

Gold was discovered in Alaska, a land of short growing season, and where at first, anyway, men had little time for anything but gold. Puget Sound was Alaska's gate, her larder, and producer-supplier of manufactured goods. Forests produced lumber for ships to carry the goods, and produced the wood for staves for the barrels in which food, nails and other goods were packed. Manufacturers and farmers prospered, and with increased rail and sea shipping, they expanded to compete in world markets.

Water that had rafted produce and bales of wool and hay to market; water that had floated log rafts and carried logs in flumes to mills, commenced an even more important role with the close of the old century and the beginning of the new. Water power. On rivers east and west, on the Spokane, Skagit, Snoqualmie and Lewis, and then on

the Columbia, dams and powerhouses rose. Turbines spinning in quiet river canyons produce electricity to power factories and to light cities miles away. Rivers became the prime energy source, attracting many new industries—producers of aluminum among them. Dams also were built to impound water for irrigation, and only secondarily to produce electricity. Some were designed for an optimum of both. Water impounded by huge Grand Coulee Dam on the Columbia irrigates tens of thousands of acres of once semi-desert, a part of a still developing scheme that ranks among the world's great land reclamation projects. Lower dams downstream from Grand Coulee created a series of lakes that step up in levels from a point near tidewater to the interior of Washington. Ship's locks around each dam, in effect, have made the Columbia an arm of the sea. Barges travel slack water to link the eastern part of the state to ocean-going freighters at tidewater ports.

Forests, and saltwater and freshwater resources, or avenues, dominated most of Washington's first hundred years as territory and state. The facts of economic life altered sharply, however, before mid-twentieth century, and especially around Puget Sound. The interest of one man in flying, and in building aircraft, catalyzed interests and energies of others. The result, tempered by events, grew into a giant aerospace industry that today dominates the Puget Sound economy, and employs a work force more than double that of the wood products industry of the entire state.

Although new technologies, in one way or another, control the working day of most persons, the forests and the saltwater and freshwater resources are increasingly occupying the leisure day.

The Coast and The Olympics

The Washington Coast is two separate worlds: the south half is best characterized as benign, the north half as wild. Two huge bays occupy most of the south. Protecting sand spits narrow the entrance to each, and create inside shorelines, that in total length, approach the length of the state's entire Pacific front. Land in the south is low-lying; its composition, soft. Over the ages the rocks were broken and eroded by the sea, broken down into sands that built up into broad beaches, dunes and long bars. Low-growing pines and taller spruce cluster in thickets on exposed points above tides and floodwater; moss-draped maples and alders stand in the lee of hummocks, and along protected, tidal reaches of rivers.

Men came to the south more than a hundred years ago, and prospered at fishing and logging. The narrow coastal plain is backed by anonymous hills, a cut-over land of forests that fell decades ago, but that now are coming back. Long stretches of lowland have standing water all year round, and in these a substantial cranberry culture thrives. The climate is delightfully mild, with summers that are never really hot, nor winters that are really cold. Many a winter will pass without a killing frost, but never will one pass without occasional stinging winds and rains that serve to heighten appreciation of the hearth and a blazing driftwood fire.

Willapa Bay and Grays Harbor are seaports shipping lumber and wood products, and are also important fishing centers. Huge Willapa has choice oyster grounds in vast shallows that are exposed at low tide. Crab, halibut, salmon, shrimp and other fish are taken commercially by boats operating out of both bays. Offshore runs of salmon are notable, and are the major sport fishing interest.

The north half of Washington's Coast is without any indentation in which to safely harbor a ship; by sea, it is a most inhospitable shore. Beaches often are narrow slabs of rock or tumbled boulders, although a goodly stretch of shore, just north of Grays Harbor, has fine, broad, sand beaches. North of that, however, are miles of shore so unchanged that they might easily be recognized by early Spanish and English seamen.

Some fifty miles of the upper north Coast is a part of Olympic National Park. A narrow strip, a mile to two miles wide, was set aside, and is connected with the main park about a dozen miles inland by a corridor of land. Olympic National Park is in the center of a seventy-by-eighty-mile peninsula bounded by the Pacific, Puget Sound and the Strait of Juan de Fuca. The heart of the park, the reason for it, are the Olympic Mountains. The Olympics are no mere *range;* they do not, for instance, stretch from *here* to *there;* they take no special direction (excepting up), follow no fault line, establish no pattern. They are a conglomerate of mountainous, magnificent disorder. Statistically, they may be unimpressive, as great mountains go. Maximum elevations fall short of

18

eight thousand feet. They do not, however, rise from a supporting shoulder, but thrust directly up from the sea. In the west and southwest, the abrupt rise of the mountains in the face of prevailing winds causes rainfall that can average more than a hundred and forty inches annually. A few miles distant, in the lee of the mountains, rainfall measuring less than twenty inches annually is common.

A visitor to Olympic National Park Shore may choose among three sections. The three are relatively similar, except for animal life. In the south, U. S. Highway 101 parallels the beach for about fifteen miles. Numerous turnouts allow a motorist to stop within a few hundred feet of the beach. The two northern sections are accessible only to those who wish to hike in. The upper of the two extends south from Cape Alava for eighteen miles to the mouth of the Quillayute River. The second extends south for fourteen miles from the Quillayute to the mouth of the Hoh River. The ends of the two north sections, although not directly accessible to vehicles, may be reached in a few minutes by trail. Hiking the Olympic Shore is sometimes like passing a great offshore ruin, a ruin of low and high rocks, of clusters of rock columns and arches. Beaches are sand, fine gravel or sometimes small boulders. Along the north sections, at the upper limits of winter's storm tides, rock or clay banks rise abruptly from the beach. Some are two to five hundred feet high, and some are virtually unscalable without special climbing equipment. Between the Hoh and Quillayute rivers the beach is often blocked by headlands that must be climbed. Trails over the headlands are steep. They cut through ten- to fifteen-foot-high thickets of salal, salmonberry and

scrub alder. It is jungle, in the strict sense, and the hiker is well-advised to stay with the beach or with blazed trails.

The difficulties of human access to the wild beaches have encouraged a rare and attractive world of animals and birds. The careful observer may see the black oystercatcher, with his long, brilliant red beak, or may see a great bald eagle drop like a rock to scoop a fish from the bay. Harbor seals are often seen swimming close inshore, and some offshore rocks are draped with the graceful forms of sea lions.

Although the Olympic Park interior contrasts sharply with the Shore, they are similar, as both are important wildlife refuges. The interior is also profoundly tempered and influenced by the nearby Pacific. From many Olympic high points one may observe one of the great phenomena of this earth. The earth's supply of water is fixed; it is used and reused in an endless cycle of evaporation and precipitation. In the Olympics one may see clouds forming above the Pacific as the cycle begins—saltwater to clouds, clouds to rain, rain to creeks and rivers, and rivers to the sea. Atop a five-thousand-foot ridge, one may see great fog banks flow into the valleys. At night, by moonlight, the fog banks seem to be an extension of the sea, a sea in which the high ridges and peaks appear as islands and peninsulas.

The Olympics are an extraordinary wilderness. In but a few miles a hiker may rise from a dark, humid rain forest to a sharp ridge in glacial chill. One may walk from the eerily silent green world of jungle to the edge of land, to the Pacific and endless breakers driving in—never calm—altering only to diminish or increase in force, or to the ebb and flood of tides.

Below: Low tide at Cape Flattery, the Olympic Peninsula's northwest tip, where the Pacific and Juan de Fuca Strait meet. Sea wrack, rockweed and eelgrass cover the rocks around pools that are a favorite hunting ground of raccoons living in the adjacent forests.

Right: An August sun casts slender shadows of beach grass on the warm, dry sands of a South Coast Washington beach. The beaches are long and broad, and despite their popularity with vacationers since the 1880's, are still tracked by wild animals and birds.

Below: A long, Pacific comber breaks on the rock-strewn shore as high tides push into a narrow cove.

Right: Seagulls, seeming so often as restless as the ocean itself, rest momentarily behind an ebbing tide.

Below: A large herd of Roosevelt elk rest on a snow field on a hot summer's day high in the mountains of Olympic National Park. Olympic elk are estimated to number about six thousand animals. They spend their summers in high country, and winters in lowland meadows and forests. Adults may weigh anywhere from seven hundred up to a thousand pounds.

Right: The road to Hurricane Ridge in the northern Olympic Peninsula—in eighteen miles it climbs to six thousand feet from sea level on Juan de Fuca Strait.

Below: Seagulls mount an Olympics headland, symbolizing, in this photograph, the interrelationships of the ocean and the great mountains that rise from it.

Right: Morning mists shroud the dense Coastal forests along the Pacific side of the Olympic Peninsula.

Below: A Columbian blacktail deer grazes a meadow on a slope near the Hurricane Ridge visitor center.

Right: The lovely avalanche fawnlily, with white petals and yellow center, follows retreating snows in early summer in Olympic Mountains high country.

Below: The Bailey Range of the Olympic Mountains photographed from Hurricane Ridge. Among areas that are easily accessible to the motorist, Hurricane Ridge has perhaps the most spectacular outlook of any section of Olympic National Park. A good road runs inland from Port Angeles on U. S. Highway 101.

Right: Soleduck Falls on Soleduck River (sometimes spelled Sol Duc) in northern Olympic National Park, is among the longest rivers on the Peninsula. Curiously, after its confluence with the Bogachiel River, the combined streams suddenly become the Quillayute River for their final, six-mile run to the Pacific.

Below: Mount Olympus, near the heart of the Olympic National Park, is actually three peaks—East, Middle and South—the highest of which rises to 7,965 feet.

Right: A moss-covered maple leans out over the shore of Lake Crescent in the northern Olympic Peninsula. U. S. Highway 101 follows the south shore of the lake. Fall mists soften colors and outlines of hills.

Below: Ocean fogs sweep into the Olympic Mountain foothills, which combined with the high annual rainfall, account for the dark, jungle-like forests.

Right: A trail shelter deep in the mountains of Olympic National Park. Many shelters, such as this one on the upper Soleduck River, are spaced along trails at about the average, one-day, back-pack hike apart.

Below: The Olympic rain forests can at times be surprisingly open at ground level, especially in stands of huge, virgin Douglas fir, Sitka spruce and Western hemlock. The dense, overhead canopy of foliage admits so little light that few but low, ground-hugging plants survive. Rain stands in pools on a carpet of moss in the high country; nearby may be fields of avalanche lilies, among the loveliest of alpine flowers.

Right: Where the deciduous maple intrudes in rain forests, undergrowth is often luxuriant; ferns and moss grow high in the trees, and mature shrubs and small trees sprout from the sides of other trees as much as thirty to forty feet above the forest floor.

37

Below: Life and death at the shore—sea plants, sea anemone and starfish crowd a tidal pool, while nearby lies a tree torn from the bank by winter's storm tides—all parts of the endless giving and taking sea.

Right: Morning fog swirls around fishing boats at Westport, Grays Harbor, as sun tries to burn through.

Below: Destruction Island, off the North Coast opposite U.S. Highway 101, is so-called from disastrous landing of an early English explorer's six-man shore party that was killed by Indians near Hoh River mouth.

Right: Morning fog obscures Neah Bay near the tip of the Olympic Peninsula on Juan de Fuca Strait. Neah Bay, a few miles in from Pacific Ocean, is the first safe anchorage on the Strait for fishing boats.

Below: Heavy winter seas break on the South Coast beaches, often covering miles of sand with foam. Cape Disappointment, with its lighthouse, is at the south end, and marks the Columbia River entrance.

Right: Offshore winds spin off the crests of great breakers rushing in toward broad, southern beaches.

Below: Salmon have been running in the Pacific off Grays Harbor; in late afternoon, a steady procession of charter boats, commercial fishermen and private boats, circle into the protected Westport anchorage.

Right: Gulls remain rock bound as storm tides pile into Beard's Hollow, near south end of Long Beach.

Below: North Head lighthouse, one of two near the Columbia's mouth, began operation in 1898. North Head is a steep promontory jutting from South Coast.

Right: The wide sands of Long Beach Peninsula sweep into the distance from North Head lighthouse.

The Lower Columbia River

The early settlement of what now is Washington was as an outpost of the British Empire. Along the Lower Columbia the British developed farms, built a fort, a village and warehouses. Their properties were operated almost as a feudal preserve, or duchy. The land they chose is an undulating corridor between two mountain ranges, and stretches from the Columbia to Puget Sound. Mile on mile of richly timbered hills spread west to the Pacific on one side, and higher hills, as heavily timbered, reach up into the Cascades on the other side. In between are green plains and valleys interlaced with streams and rivers. The area, because of its general alignment with Puget Sound, is sometimes called the Puget Trough. Foothills from the bordering ranges intrude into the corridor, although motoring through it today, one really is unaware that it is not a continuous valley. Actually, it is divided into three watersheds: the south empties into the Columbia; the middle empties into the Pacific; the north empties into Puget Sound.

It was pleasant country, most notable perhaps, for an absence of extremes. Beavers populated small streams the length of the Corridor and mink and muskrat were plentiful. In the hills for miles around were bear, deer and elk. The North American fur trade in the early 1800s was enormously lucrative. From the Great Lakes to the Pacific, a near monopoly of that trade was held by an organization named, formally, *Governor and Company of Adventurers of England trading into Hudson's Bay*. In the West, from earliest times, the Puget Corridor had been a natural highway between the Columbia River and Puget Sound. The country eminently suited the needs of Hudson's Bay Company as a southwest headquarters. In 1824 they established Fort Vancouver on the north bank of the Lower Columbia. The location had many natural advantages. It was accessible to ocean transport, was central to country rich in fur-bearing animals, and was adjacent to land that could be farmed so that the colony might be self-supporting. Also—and not at all incidentally—the location would strengthen British claims to the country north of the Columbia. Fort Vancouver grew rapidly, and the Company farms soon extended north into the Cowlitz River valley. They planted large acreages to wheat and vegetables, set out orchards, and established herds of livestock. They built a sawmill and within a decade

were exporting lumber. Indians brought salmon from the great runs in the Columbia.

The economy of the region today is different only in degree. Great log rafts still move along the Columbia to giant mills that produce pulp, paper, lumber and plywood. The fleets of salmon fishing boats and the packing plants are now concentrated just within the mouth of the Columbia, and the numbers of commercial fishing boats are matched by sport fishing boats. River bottom land and prairies support large herds of dairy and beef cattle. Wheat is no longer the important crop, but has been surplanted by feed crops for livestock. The Columbia, so important in the past, is still so now. Barges bring wheat from east of the Cascades to be stored for transshipment in tall, concrete silos along the lower river. Malting, and aluminum production about round out manufacturing.

Motoring north along the corridor today, one's general impression of the countryside is much as it would have been a century ago—of the same absence of extremes, of forested foothills reaching to the horizon. The Lewis and Kalama rivers appear eternally placid. Yellow blossoms of pond lilies cover the surface of quiet backwaters. The Indians called the pond lily *wokas,* and for them the pod was an important food source. Along a cliff top, the peeling, orange-red trunks of madrona trees stand out against the black-green foliage of Douglas fir and hemlock. Handsome cattle graze lush, green meadows. Soon the Cowlitz River slides smoothly by, and later, the Chehalis, on its way to the Pacific. Farms are not large, but are modestly prosperous. The highway easily mounts low, intervening hills, and the orientation now, as it always has been, is more toward the north, toward Puget Sound.

Below: Ruins of an old salmon cannery on piling a few miles upstream from the Pacific. The Columbia estuary, here, is as much as five to nine miles wide.

Right: The quiet waters at Ilwaco, just within the mouth of the Columbia, have sheltered fishermen and their boats from storms for more than a century.

Below: A covered bridge crosses the small tributary Grays River in a quiet valley of Wahkiakum County.

Right: Columbia Lancaster, Washington's first, elected territorial representative to the U.S. Congress, built this house in the 1850's near the confluence of the Lewis and Columbia rivers. It is a remarkable house for its day, both for its faithfulness to the Classic Revival style, and for such wild and remote country, where the average houses, at best, were of logs.

Below: A man and his dogs walk beside a private lake, that, as a tidal backwater of the lower Columbia, was part of important Indian fishing grounds. Trails of Hudson's Bay trappers passed nearby.

Right: Steep rocks and still, deep water make the Lewis River above Lucia Falls an ideal swimming river.

Below: Wheat from east of the Cascades is barged down the Columbia to the Port of Vancouver to be stored awaiting transshipment to ports of the world.

Right: Autumn mists hang in the hills and over the placid river, stretches of which are little changed since Hudson's Bay men paddled upstream and down.

Right: The Kalama River, which rises in the Cascades west of Mount St. Helens, is an important salmon and steelhead fishing stream. Its lower reaches, before its confluence with the Columbia, are tidal.

Puget Sound Region

Among intriguing natural phenomena in America is Puget Sound. The interest of many inland seas is brutish, awesome. Not Puget. The Sound, for all its broad reaches, is more intimate, more in tune with man as an individual, much as a series of smaller lakes would be, with secluded bays and uninhabited islands. The Sound, essentially, is a great basin, about forty miles wide at its broadest, into which is inserted a wide, arrowhead-shaped peninsula with its point in the north. It is a jagged arrowhead, this Kitsap Peninsula, chipped and notched with small bays and inlets.

The designation, *Puget Sound,* is actually inaccurate, as commonly used. But it is more convenient than specifying the individual parts, such as Haro Strait, Rosario Strait, Juan de Fuca Strait or Admiralty Inlet. Juan de Fuca Strait and Hood Canal are usually designated properly. Hood Canal is a long, narrow arm of water that forms the west and southwest parts of arrowhead-shaped Kitsap Peninsula. The Canal is not a *canal* in the sense that our current usage gives it, which usually means a man-made channel of water, but in the now-obsolete sense of any watercourse or channel. But Hood *Canal* it remains. With this exception, all further references to *Puget Sound* are intended to include all waters from its southernmost tip north to Canada, a straight-line distance of about a hundred and fifty miles.

An average width of broader reaches of the Sound is probably less than ten miles; Hood Canal averages less than two miles. In cruising the Sound it seems there must be an island for everyone. The San Juan Archipelago in the north is supposed to number more than a hundred and seventy islands, although most are tiny, of an acre to three in extent. Whidby Island, just south,

is about fifty miles long, but is usually little more than two or so miles wide. Other islands and numerous attenuated peninsulas further constrict the main channels, and form long, narrow passages. It has been estimated that there are more than two thousand miles of saltwater shoreline, including islands.

Annual rainfall in the Sound area will vary from somewhere around twenty inches in the north, to around forty in the south. Temperatures are uniformly mild. Summers are neither excessively warm, nor winters excessively cold.

Generally, the surrounding land is hilly or mountainous. Along the west shore of Hood Canal, the Olympic mountains rise abruptly for several thousand feet, eventually, a few miles inland, rising to more than five thousand feet. Along much of the canal, and around much of the Sound, continuous embankments and cliffs rise a dozen to three or four hundred feet. Principal exceptions are the wide bottom lands near the mouths of rivers, especially those on the eastern shore of the Sound.

The eastern mainland was being settled rapidly by the 60s and 70s of the last century. The Hudson's Bay Company, which earlier had established Fort Vancouver in the south extension of the Puget Corridor, founded a similar post at Nisqually, near the south tip of the Sound, in 1833. It chose rich

farm land on which to settle, and within eight years had such surpluses of goods that it was exporting beef cattle, butter, cheese and other fresh products. Company managers were educated and often brilliant men. During their short stay they introduced new varieties of grains, grasses, fruits, berries, livestock and poultry. They knew the local soils, and had stocks of implements. Then, determination of the United States-Canada boundary opened the Puget region freely to American settlers. Hudson's Bay men and their experience, and the availability of seeds, implements and animals, were invaluable to the newly arriving Americans. Although British domination had inhibited earlier American settlements, their legacy of experience spurred later development. Men settled in the broad, fertile valleys south and east of the Sound along the Nisqually, Puyallup, Snoqualmie, Snohomish, Stillaguamish, Skagit and Nooksack rivers. Sandy, silt loams and alluvial soils became valuable crop or grazing land. Dairy farming and livestock farming was the major agricultural activity, and remains much the same today. Early farm activities for cash, were almost exclusively limited to raising sheep, hogs, horses and cattle, which could be driven to market. Vegetables and fruit, now such important crops on the Puget Plains, were grown, in earlier times, mostly for home use only. Important and very early dairy farms were established in the northeast and north parts of the Olympic Peninsula in the Chimicum Valley and on the Dungeness-Sequim coastal plain.

The moist deltas and plains of the Eastern Sound were essential for the growing cities at deepwater anchorages. In the hills behind the farms was the timber that fed the mills that fed lumber to ships at these anchorages.

Mills also supplied lumber to shipyards that built ships for transporting goods, and for boats of a commercial fishing fleet. Fishermen returned to the ports with salmon and halibut. In an ever-broadening circle the varied elements of the economy of the Sound crossed over and interacted. Fish were processed and then packed for shipment in products of the lumber mills, and ships calling for cattle, lumber and fish bought additional farm products for their return journeys. Completion of the transcontinental railroad extended a commercial arm into the center of the United States and beyond. The opening of trade with Alaska extended another arm. More and more ships came into Puget Sound, and on Commencement Bay, Elliott Bay, Port Gardner Bay and Bellingham Bay, more and more docks and warehouses were built. The bays became the principal centers of commerical activity, and population patterns were stabilized into what, essentially, they are today.

The five principal cities of the east shore, and environs, between them now share the major portion of the state's population. Inhabitants of these cities are unlikely to pass a day without a view of the Sound, of busy comings and goings of ferryboats and tugs, of freighters heavy in the water with cargo. White sails of sloop or ketch tack across a bay that shows a great sweeping curve of tide rip. Off in the distance may be a wooded island, perhaps with a ring of sand circling a quiet cove. A side of the island may have rock slabs sheering directly into the deep, or a beach of white, shining, quartz pebbles. A barely perceptible tide, or current, rattles the pebbles. Offshore, a seal's sleek, bullet-shaped head soundlessly breaks the surface, breathes out and breathes in, and soundlessly slips below.

Below: Private boats and one commercial fishing boat cluster around a dock at the town of Hoodsport, on Hood Canal. The Canal is not a *canal*, as such, but is a long, narrow, salt-water arm reaching south from the meeting of Juan de Fuca Strait and Puget Sound between the Olympic and the Kitsap Peninsulas.

Right: Capitol Buildings of Olympia, seat of government of the State of Washington, are seen here across tidal basin of Budd Inlet, southern tip of Puget Sound.

Below: Fort Nisqually, on Puget Sound, was Hudson's Bay Company headquarters on the Sound until after determination of the United States-Canada boundary; here is a portion of a reconstruction-restoration of old Fort Nisqually, in Tacoma's Point Defiance Park.

Right: Hood Canal has no major cities or towns; the shores are mostly given to vacation resorts, homes; waterskiing and fishing are the common activities.

Below: Four-thousand-foot-high Mount Si is the motorist's first close-up Cascade view going east from Puget Sound on Interstate 90 to Snoqualmie Pass.

Right: The Narrows Bridge, Tacoma, connects the Eastshore Sound with the Kitsap and Olympic Peninsulas and Hood Canal. In the distance, seeming to be a part of the horizon clouds, is Mount Rainier.

Below: A field of daffodils in the Puyallup Valley, with Mount Rainier in the distance—the largest share of the nation's flower bulbs are grown in Washington, and most of these are grown in the Puyallup Valley.

Right: Tiny, near-landlocked Gig Harbor is across Puget Sound Narrows from the north tip of Tacoma.

Below: Two mammoth cranes load container cargo on the ship, "Hawaiian Farmer"; in background are Elliott Bay and the waterfront of downtown Seattle.

Right: The Space Needle rises high above Seattle Center, formerly the site of the Century 21 World's Fair, in 1962. The Fair site is now an entertainment center, with an opera house, repertory theater, coliseum, science center, parks and gardens. A monorail line connects the Center and downtown Seattle area.

Below: Seattle encircles Elliott Bay, at right; in the immediate foreground is Seattle Center; beyond it, is downtown Seattle; on horizon is Mount Rainier.

Right: Visitors may take an elevator to a restaurant or observation gallery atop Seattle's Space Needle, shown here framed by arches of the Science Center.

Below: The City of Seattle occupies a long, narrow piece of land between Puget Sound-Elliott Bay (foreground) and Lake Union (upper right) and eighteen-mile-long Lake Washington, out of the photo (right).

Right: At night, lighted fountains play in the water gardens of Pacific Science Center in Seattle Center.

Below: Mists rise as a winter morning's sun warms an upland valley near Mount Rainier; tails of spray rise behind unlimited hydroplanes in Seattle's annual, summer, Seafair races on Lake Washington; children splash in the water off a San Juan Islands beach.

Right: Commutors park cars (upper left) at ferryboat terminal at Winslow, Bainbridge Island, for short run across Puget Sound to downtown Seattle terminal.

Below: Sheltered inlet at Port Madison on Bainbridge Island—Bainbridge is one of two large islands that are within reasonable commuting distance of Seattle.

Right: Fishermen empty nets on the upper Sound; salmon migrate to spawning grounds in the many rivers entering Puget Sound; the numbers of fish taken by net during the commercial fishing season support a substantial canning and packing industry.

Below: Seattle is built on a series of steep hills, and a view of the city and of water is almost as common as the water itself; the city view, here, is from the side of Queen Anne Hill in the early evening.

Right: The Indian name for Mount Rainier is Tahoma —Tahoma the Mountain, dwelling place of the gods, so it seems it might be, as seen from Vashon Island.

Below: Seattle—a downtown office building flashes in the sunlight; unlimited hydroplanes reach speeds of about 150 mph during Seafair races; a ketch rides at anchor off a private dock on Lake Washington.

Right: Late evening light silhouettes a wind-bent spruce on Lopez, third largest of the San Juan Islands.

Below: Hood Canal Floating Bridge takes Highway 104 across north end of the canal, connecting the Kitsap Peninsula with Highway 101 and the Olympic Peninsula; Olympic Mountains are on the skyline.

Right: The old tower at Fort Worden, Port Townsend, at the northeast tip of the Olympic Peninsula, is a brick mason's showpiece; old Fort Worden, now abandoned, was once a part of the United States coastal defense system; tower is a private residence.

Below: Deception Pass, from Deception Pass State Park—the Pass is a narrow, high-walled, turbulant, tidal passage between the north tip of Whidbey Island and Fidalgo Island in northern Puget Sound.

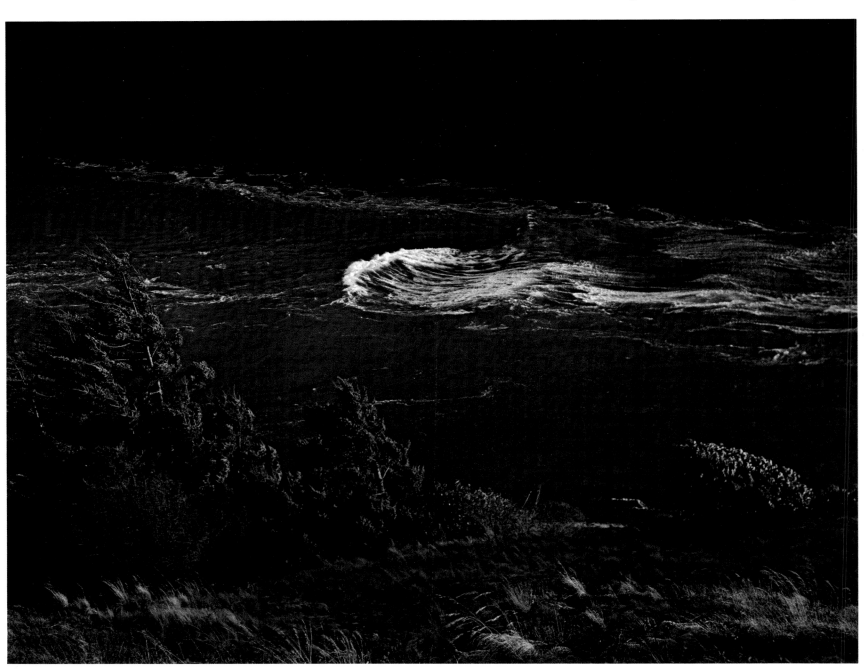

Right: Madrona tree on Orcas Island, in the San Juans —the madrona (or Pacific madrone—Arbutus menziesi) comes near to being a waterside trademark of Puget Sound, often growing to the edge of high tide.

Below: A freighter runs north heading for the Olympic Peninsula tip, where, without stopping, it will turn west to the Pacific through Juan de Fuca Strait. Once, at that Port Townsend juncture, all ships cleared customs, and Port Townsend was a prosperous city. Her citizens believed her to be the future, great city of the Pacific. Handsome buildings were built of brick and of stone; mansions were built on the heights; but the dream failed to materialize, and the city declined. It is now, quite possibly, the best preserved nineteenth century town in the state. The turreted Hastings residence, and St. Paul's Episcopal Church (built in 1865) typify the charming town.

Right: Harvested oats near Mt. Vernon—the fertile delta plains of the eastern Sound support hay and feed crops for dairy and beef cattle, and together are the major agricultural activity, with commercial vegetable, berry, poultry and egg production following.

Below: Islands for an idyll—so the San Juans often seem. Delightful, tiny McConnell Island would appear to satisfy most any man's longing to get away from it all, where he might walk along a silent beach.

Right: The San Juans are rocky, and obtaining an adequate supply of fresh water is often a problem for those who would live there. The San Juans are in the Olympic Mountains rain shadow, and rainfall is markedly less than that of most of the Sound region.

Right: Morning mists rise as fishermen set out downstream on the Stillaguamish River, north of Everett.

Below: A tiny tug maneuvers logs in Port Angeles harbor. Douglas fir cones—cones are gathered for their seed to replant cut-over land. Wild rhododendrons bloom along Hood Canal; the native rhododendron is common in the forests around the Canal, and in spring, especially near Port Townsend, one may see them for miles along the main highways.

Right: Log rafts at Port Angeles near one of several large mills on the north shore of Olympic Peninsula.

Below: A log raft moves out of Deception Pass. Log blockhouse, a relic of the comic, American-English Pig War for possession of the San Juan Islands a century ago—the blockhouse, on big San Juan Island, is now a part of a National Historical Park. Puget Sound Indian tribes compete in a race of dugout, war canoes, a part of annual Lummi Indian water festival.

Right: Purse seine fishermen in summer maneuver across the salmon banks south of San Juan Island.

Below: Mount Baker and the North Cascades photographed from summit of Mt. Constitution in Moran State Park on Orcas Island, largest of San Juan group.

Right: San Juan Island purse seiners—most of their catch goes to canneries in Anacortes, Friday Harbor.

Cascade Mountains

The Cascades might be likened to a garden wall, in which garden and wall are one. They are forested with dense stands of fir, hemlock, cedar and pine to about five thousand feet elevation, then are more open, trees dwindling gradually to stunted clusters, until ultimately, between six and seven thousand feet, they reach the limit of their existence. In lower elevations, rhododendrons are common and often dominate the forest understory, their shapes less bunched and more attenuated than their cultivated cousins, as they reach upward for sunlight. Wherever the masses of interlaced conifer branches part to permit sunlight to enter, or in meadows and glades, the ground may be blue with lupine or yellow with the daisy-like mule ears. In the shadows nearby may be the white blossoms of the lovely ground dogwood. On the heights, cliffs may be red with penstemon or rose-pink with heather, and fields may be blue, yellow and magenta with mountain lupine, glacier lilies and Indian paintbrush. In the highest meadows the delicate, white, avalanche lily blooms at the edge of retreating snows. The magnificent garden is also a super wall.

The Cascades are really two ranges—an older, lower formation, with newer, higher individual peaks standing on the old foundation. Elevations of the older range average near five thousand feet; the newer, the great individual peaks, stand from eight to fourteen thousand feet. The new peaks are volcanic (now dormant), that over the ages built up to the forms we now know.

The range extends south from Canada for about seven hundred miles. Two rivers only cut through the Cascades: the Columbia, which forms most of Washington's southern boundary, and the Klamath River, near the southern terminous of the range. The Cascades rise inland from the Pacific at a distance, generally, of about a hundred miles. In the north they are nearer the Coast because of the deep, eastward penetration of Juan de Fuca Strait and Puget Sound.

In the north is the Cascades' greatest, general uplift. Nowhere along their length do they approach such ruggedness combined with height. The region is among the great mountain wildernesses. In 1968, the 505,000-acre North Cascade National Park

was established. Adjoining it is a 169,000-acre National Recreation Area, and two Wilderness Areas. A wilderness designation, as now written in federal law, is only limited protection, because it does allow unlimited mining, be it tunnel or open pit.

North Cascades peaks hold more than a hundred and fifty active glaciers, moving, grinding away, honing ridges, sharpening peaks. The high annual precipitation brings as much as five hundred inches of snow in winter. In the high meadows, spring, summer and fall are compressed into about three months. As the prevailing winds bearing moisture are from the west, east slope precipitation is markedly lower. Forests change from fir to pine, and at lower elevations the land is semi-desert. Virtually all of the Cascade high country and much of the middle elevations and foothills are federally owned. They are administered by either the U. S. Forest Service or National Park Service.

North, Middle, and South Cascade regions differ. The North has a certain savagery and sense of power. Man's ego is dampened. Great amphitheatric cirques high above tree line have that curious silence of the heights where even a sudden light breeze is startling, and the sound of a trickle of pebbles dislodged by a boot can seem deafening.

Mount Rainier and Mount Rainier National Park dominate the Middle Cascades. Rainier is totally different from the North Cascades—if one excepts Mount Baker. Rainier is the *great*, the *mammoth* mountain. A trail encircling it near timberline is ninety miles long. It has more than two dozen active glaciers, of which at least half have been classed as major. Emmons Glacier, the largest, is about four miles long, by about a mile wide. Glaciers are composed of successive layers of snow compacted to ice,

sometimes to a thickness of several hundred feet. So great does the weight become, that on steep slopes, the mass slides slowly downhill, grinding and tearing the soil beneath it. Movements up to a foot and more a day have been recorded. Six of Mount Rainier's glaciers originate at the summit. Each winter, new snows pile up to replace and compact the layer below. Each year the glaciers grind down the mountain, pushing masses of boulders before them. In such a manner has Rainier been carved over the millennia. Shoulders buttressing the main mountain are minor mountain ranges in themselves. Nowhere, in all of the Cascades, does one sense mass of such sheer, overwhelming immensity.

The Washington Cascades south of Rainier are far less precipitous than the Central and North Cascades — with three notable exceptions. The Goat Rocks, immediately south of Rainier, might be called a North Cascades in miniature, but miniature in area, not in heights. Mere *Rocks* seem something of an understatement for a cluster of peaks and ridges that rise to elevations of seven and eight thousand feet. South of Goat Rocks are Mount St. Helens and Mount Adams, one near the west edge, the other near the east edge of the older, lower Cascades. Each has a distinct, an individual profile: Adams, somewhat sprawling, with the brutality of a Rainier; St. Helens, a thing of symmetry and grace.

South from St. Helens and Adams, the Cascades decline into foothills that are less than five thousand feet elevation. Gradually the land falls away. River valleys tributary to the Columbia intervene. The Washington Cascades terminate abruptly at the Columbia in a deep, steep-sided gorge, with occasional near-vertical, thousand-foot cliffs.

Right: Snowgrass Creek tumbles down a rock-strewn slope in Goat Rocks Wilderness in Central Cascades.

Below: Mount Baker, in the North Cascades, in Mount Baker National Forest, rises to elevation 10,750 feet. A dormant volcano, reliable early reports state that Baker strewed the countryside with ashes in 1842.

Right: North Cascades from Kulshan Ridge in the Mount Baker ski area—it is accessible from Highway 542, sixty miles east of Bellingham on the Sound.

Below: The hoary marmot is a common, often-observed, high-country animal. They live in rocky areas, and are among the largest of rodents, their tail-and-body length reaching thirty inches. They have a shrill, piercing whistle that can be heard for great distances. North Cascades National Park—near Mount Logan more than twenty streams pour down slopes into a glacial basin, to merge and become the source of Bridge Creek. Downstream, the icy waters of Bridge Creek swirl around a boulder.

Right: Dwarf mimulus, or monkey flower, is one of the many, brilliant wild flowers of the high Cascades.

Below: Mount Shuksan (elevation 9,127 feet) photographed from Kulshan Ridge, Mount Baker ski area.

Right: Glacier Peak (elevation 10,541 feet) is shown from Miner's Ridge, near Image Lake, in the four-hundred-seventy-thousand-acre Glacier Peak Wilderness, south of the North Cascades National Park.

Below: Wild flowers bloom on a hillside above the Paradise Loop Road in Mount Rainier National Park. In the background is Tatoosh Range with Unicorn Peak near center, and Castle and Pinnacle Peaks, right.

Right: In autumn, Larch trees (tamarack) turn color near Perfection Lake in the Enchantment Lakes Basin of the Stuart Range, an Eastcentral Cascades spur. Prusig Peak and The Temple rise behind the lake.

Below: Cloud-capped Big Four Mountain is in the Monte Cristo Range of the Cascade Mountains east of the important Puget Sound lumber city of Everett.

Right: A pack string traverses a slope on the Miner's Ridge trail to Image Lake in Glacier Peak Wilderness.

Below: The Western Washington forests can be unbelievably dense; few great, unbroken expanses still exist—as seen here—except in the national parks.

Right: Edith Creek falls down the south slopes of Mount Rainier (elevation 14,408 feet) near Paradise Inn and Visitor Center in Mount Rainier National Park.

Below: It is understandable that the North Cascades have for so long been virtually impenetrable, even on foot. They now are a part of North Cascades National Park; Eldorado Peak is on the near skyline, left.

Right: A skier at Crystal Mountain, northeast of Mount Rainier (background), in the Central Cascades.

122

Below: Ice cave in Paradise Glacier on Mount Rainier —Paradise Glacier is dead, no longer moving, and a combination of summer ice-melt underneath the glacier, and the passage of warm air through surface breaks, has formed caves. Flood-lighted slopes permit night skiing at Snoqualmie Pass in the Central Cascades fifty miles from Seattle. Ski class in the Mount Baker ski area tries a beginners' slope with the sunlit summit of Mount Shuksan in the background.

Right: A double-chair lift takes skiers up the slopes at White Pass—Mount Rainier is in the background.

Below: High on a shoulder of Mount Adams the twisted, derelict form of a long-dead tree still holds out against the elements. Great clumps of squaw grass with creamy-white heads brighten upland slopes in early summer. Twin fawns hide in a forest glade.

Right: Eagle Falls on Skykomish River—the Cascades are aptly named; streams almost without number rush down the slopes in near-continuous cascades.

Below: The symmetrical cone of Mount St. Helens—elevation 9,671 feet—suggests to geologists that, alone among the Cascades volcanos, its formation was postglacial. In the distance is Mount Adams.

Right: Mount St. Helens from Spirit Lake—reliable reports tell of a heavy ash fall from St. Helens in 1852, and of the eruption of a basalt flow occurring in 1854.

Below: Climbers explore seracs and crevasses in the Toutle Glacier ice falls on Mount St. Helens. Stalagmites and stalactites of ice glitter in a lava cave near Mount Adams. Trout Lake, below Mount Adams, seems the compleat lake for compleat anglers.

Right: Spirit Lake, elevation 3,199 feet, on the north side of Mount St. Helens, is among the largest of the natural lakes on the western Cascades slopes.

Below: A Cascades stream—annual precipitation along the west slopes of the Cascades is often more than a hundred inches. Much of it falls as snow that feeds the many streams during the long, dry summers.

Below: A Cascades stream—annual precipitation along the west slopes of the Cascades is often more than a hundred inches. Much of it falls as snow that feeds the many streams during the long, dry summers.

Right: In autumn, the leaves of vine maple color great stretches of Douglas fir, hemlock and cedar forests a brilliant yellow-orange and red-orange.

Below: The ancient Columbia cut into the land at near the same rate that the Cascades rose, creating the great gorge where mountains and river meet.

Right: Ponderosa pine at the edge of the Columbia River—the east-slope Cascades are drier; forests are more open, and pine rather than fir predominate.

Below: Table Mountain rears up for thirty-four hundred feet above Columbia River near Bonneville Dam.

Below: Table Mountain rears up for thirty-four hundred feet above Columbia River near Bonneville Dam.

Right: Land suitable for farming occasionally borders the Columbia as it cuts through the Cascades, but mostly the land is too steep for anything but trees.

Below: A storm moves up the Columbia Gorge toward orchards in bloom near town of White Salmon.

Right: Sheer basalt shafts at Cape Horn demonstrate the great force of the ancient rising of the Cascades.

Below: High on a shoulder of Mount Adams the twisted, derelict form of a long-dead tree still holds out against the elements. Great clumps of squaw grass with creamy-white heads brighten upland slopes in early summer. Twin fawns hide in a forest glade.

Right: Eagle Falls on Skykomish River—the Cascades are aptly named; streams almost without number rush down the slopes in near-continuous cascades.

Below: A riverboat pushes two oil-filled barges to an upstream Columbia port. The separate housing atop the barges will be loaded with wheat for return trip.

Right: Nineteen-hundred-foot-high Wind Mountain rises virtually from the shore of the Columbia River.

East of the Cascades

Washington, east of the Cascades, is desert and scab rock; it is seemingly endless orchards and high, undulating, grain-covered hills; it is broad, irrigated fields of potatoes and sugar beets. Cattle graze lowland meadows and upland range lands. In the North, and in the Southeast corner, mountains rise to five and six thousand feet —a high country of open, pine forests. Through all of it runs a great river and its tributaries, watering the fields, lighting the cities, powering the industries, and freighting the raw materials and products.

The Methow, Wenatchee and Yakima rivers fall down the Cascade Mountain east slopes into the Columbia. Their lengths reflect the transition of West to East, of forest to desert. The East lacks the softness of the West; the East is more often hard; contrasts are sharp. That which the land provides is given reluctantly, and only with encouragement. A lizard may rush through hot, dry dust beneath sagebrush only a yard from fields of rich, green grass.

The shape of the land is immensely varied. If it were possible to generalize at all, one might say that it is a crescent encircling a basin—with the open end of the crescent in the south. It moves north past the east-slope Cascades, swings into the North and Northeast, and then falls south. It is highly irregular in form, and is a mixture of forests, mountains, plateaus, channeled scab land, lowland and highland valleys, and rolling hills. Within the irregular crescent—and again, speaking generally—is the Columbia Basin. Valleys slice across the crescent and spill into the basin. The basin is almost as varied as the crescent, with descending plains, intruding ridges, and deep, steep-walled coulees. The coulees were formed ages ago when ice-age rivers cut across the

land. The crescent and the basin are drained by the Columbia River. The Columbia's tributaries were the sites of early settlement.

The first permanent White settlement in Washington was near its present, eastern margin. Spokane House was established in 1810, by men of the North West Company, on a site sixty miles up the Spokane River from its confluence with the Columbia. The North West Company was a combination of Scottish-Canadian traders, and their object was the fur trade. They soon had rivals in an American firm, the Pacific Fur Company;

they bought them out, and then themselves disappeared, in a few years, into the organization of Hudson's Bay Company.

Traffic in furs is the story, largely, of the following half-century. Hudson's Bay Company influence, however, waned after settlement in 1846 of the United States-Canada boundary. Then too, the fur trade itself was dwindling, as numbers of wild animals were depleted. Still, Indian unrest inhibited permanent settlement. A Christian missionary party had settled in the valley of the Walla Walla River earlier, but until the late 1850s, military and fur-trading posts were virtually the only White habitations east of the Cascades. The change came with an American military victory over the Indians, and then with the discovery of gold.

North and east of the Walla Walla Valley are the Bitterroot Mountains. A gold strike near the Clearwater River on the western slopes of the Bitterroots attracted thousands of miners and prospectors. The Walla Walla area was a natural gateway to the mine fields for transshipment of food and supplies from Lower Columbia sources. Materiel came up the Columbia and was transferred to land transport for the trek to the gold fields. The high prices charged for freighting up the river, and the prices of food particularly, encouraged development of local crops. As a result, interest in food crops increased, and gradually families took up residence in the Southeast. Lands were found that were especially suitable for wheat farming, and a new and growing market for the wheat was discovered west of the Cascades. The Columbia River, so important as an avenue of commerce to the fur traders, reassumed its importance for the shipment of farm produce. Consequently, by the 1870s, the Walla Walla region was Washington's most important agricultural area, with a population nearly equal to that of Puget Sound.

Aside from the Southeast, population patterns east of the Cascades were not permanently established until the final quarter of the century. Completion of the Western portions of the transcontinental railroads quite literally made the towns that now are the principal cities. The lines crossed the State's east boundary at several points north of center. They then converged, and after doing so, split again to cross the state and pass the Cascades via four separate routes.

Population concentrations, east of the Cascades, are near the west, east and south margins on these routes. The vast center of the state was for years largely vacant, undisturbed, except for the Columbia River.

The Columbia, in very early times, had cut a steep-walled gorge through Central Washington. More than two million acres of potentially productive land lay idle for lack of water. The high lift from river level made irrigation economically unfeasible. Completion of Grand Coulee Dam—begun in the 1930s—and implementation of the Columbia Basin Irrigation Project, is returning the land to life.

Essential to any land reclamation project are reservoirs for storage of surplus water. The Columbia, and the melting, ice-age glaciers, cut numerous channels. The Columbia's original, ancient course, cut deep into the land, was one. During the chaotic millennia of the ice-age melt, others were cut. The great glaciers dammed the ancient Columbia channel, forcing the river to alter its course and cut a new gorge. After the eventual retreat of the continental ice sheet, the Columbia returned to its former channel —that which, essentially, we know today. The ice-age gulch that the diverted Columbia had carved— the Grand Coulee—was left standing dry. Other coulees had also been cut east of the Cascades as dams impounding glacier lakes gave way, and repeated, mighty floods swept across the country. Grand Coulee, from which the Dam takes its name, averages about six hundred feet deep, from two to six miles wide, and is more than fifty miles long. As Banks Lake, the Grand Coulee now serves the reclamation project.

The Columbia Basin Project is only a part of the Central-Eastern Washington story in the twentieth century, a story that basically is one of water—water for power, and water for irrigation. The Tieton River Reservoir, deep in the Cascades, waters more than twenty-seven thousand acres. Tens of thousands of additional acres are either being irrigated, or being planned for irrigation, along all of the tributary systems of the Columbia. In adddition, all provide a measure of flood control, or generate power, or do both. Nuclear power, generated at the giant Hanford plant at Richland, further expands the picture, and adds nuclear-related, scientific activities to the yet unrealized potential of Eastern Washington.

Below: Aspen have turned yellow when cowboys drive herds of hereford cattle from high, summer range down into the Okanogan ranch country. A rodeo rider at the Omak Stampede, the highlight of which is the *Suicide Race* downhill into and across Okanogan River.

Right: Aspen leaves against the sun in autumn seem to be of transparent gold. Aspen groves are scattered through high country pine forests especially.

Below: Sagebrush along the Columbia—once it grew rife, but is disappearing as water reclaims the land.

Right: Fifty-five-mile-long Lake Chelan penetrates the heart of the eastern slope of the Cascades. Regular boat service connects the upper and lower lake.

Below: In autumn, waters of the Wenatchee River reflect the yellow and yellow-orange of vine maple.

Right: Delicious apples leave an orchard in the Yakima Valley. The valleys along the base of the Cascade east slopes are renowned for tree fruit.

Below: The Yakima River (left) cuts through high hills between Ellensburg and Yakima. Interstate Highway 90 bridges the Columbia (upper photograph) at Vantage. Sheep still graze Eastern Washington range land, although their numbers are declining.

Right: Interstate Highway 90 follows the upper Yakima River through the east slope Cascade foothills; in the background is the Stuart Range of the Cascades.

Below: Lake Chelan is fifteen hundred feet deep at its deepest—four hundred feet below sea level. The upper lake is included in the Lake Chelan National Recreation Area; adjoins North Cascades National Park. Bull elk on a ridge guard a herd in the Oak Creek Game refuge in the eastern Cascade foothills.

Right: The Methow (say Met-how) River rises in the Northeast Cascades, and runs through country largely devoted to feed crops and beef cattle production.

Right: Mount Adams, elevation 12,307 feet, rises above the ranch country of the Southcentral region.

Below: Winter wheat shows the faintest traces of green in the Klickitat Valley below Mount Adams.

Right: Entire hillsides in springtime along the mid-Columbia River are often covered with lupine.

Below: Irrigated fields between Ephrata and Quincy —a network of canals carries Columbia River water from reservoirs to the once-dry lands of the Basin.

Right: The upper Columbia in Washington—near Northport, near the Canadian border, the river has not yet reached the upper limits of Coulee Dam's one-hundred-fifty-one-mile-long Lake Roosevelt.

Below: Grand Coulee Dam (left) impounds water that then is pumped into Banks Lake storage reservoir in the Grand Coulee. At Summer Falls, water from Banks Lake pours into one of a number of secondary reservoirs, to eventually irrigate fields via sprinklers.

Right: The great man-made wonder, Grand Coulee Dam—the Dam is 4,173 feet long, and 550 feet high, about equivalent to the height of a fifty-story building. In the background is Banks Lake reservoir.

Below: Spokane is the commercial center of Eastern Washington, and the largest city east of the Cascades. Water lilies bloom in a pond in Spokane's Manito Park. The Spokane River tumbles through the center of the city. Although basically always a distribution center, manufacturing is increasing in Spokane, especially aluminum production, attracted by the ready availability of electric power. Transcontinental railroads converge in Spokane, and then go their separate ways west across the state to the Pacific.

Right: The Palouse River drops over lava cliffs to empty into the Snake River at the southern margin of the rich wheat lands of the rolling, Palouse Hills.

Below: Contrasts are often sharp east of the Cascade Mountains where green fields give way to rimrock and desert slopes. Horses graze along shores of Lake Lenore in the Grand Coulee, an ancient Columbia course.

Right: Basalt columns and cliffs of Wallula Gap— near the cities of Pasco, Kennewick and Richland, the Columbia at last ends its southern course, pushes through Wallula and heads west toward the Pacific.

Below: Wheat ranch in winter near Dayton—the far Southeast, along the Touchet-Walla Walla River systems, was the earliest, extensively developed agricultural region in Washington east of the Cascades.

Right: The Grande Ronde River Canyon—in the extreme Southeast, the Grande Ronde cuts through the Blue Mountains which rise to elevations of more than six thousand feet. Lava flows along the Grand Ronde are sometimes in excess of three thousand feet thick.

Below: Washington State University (Bryan Hall, left) is at Pullman near the heart of the Palouse wheat country. Beef cattle (upper photograph) graze in a field beside a sugar beet refinery near Moses Lake. Huge Potholes Reservoir (lower photograph) is a part of the Columbia Basin Reclamation Project.

Right: A Bureau of Reclamation staff member photographs the interior of one of the huge syphons that carry Columbia River water to points in the Basin.

Below: The Palouse Hills from Steptoe Butte—the soil in the Palouse country is highly retentive of moisture and of great fertility. It is largely wind-blown loess, brought in as dust in a past age, and deposited in a layer as much as a hundred and fifty feet thick. Wheat is the major crop, followed by barley, dry field peas and beef cattle production.

Right: A combine harvests ripe wheat in the Sky-rocket Hills north of Waitsburg in the Southeast.

Washington at Random

Below: Large and small granite boulders strew the path of Buck Creek in the North Cascades. Moss-covered granite slabs edge the banks crowded with sword ferns, vine maple, hemlock and Douglas fir.

Right: A glass fish-net float from Japan rests on a Washington beach. Floats, torn from nets of Japanese fishermen by storms and tides, ride currents for five thousand miles to the eastern Pacific shore. They vary in diameter from about four inches to twenty inches and more, and in color from green to blue-green.

Below: Winter at Parkland Meadows and the Tatoosh Range in Mount Rainier National Park. The Tatoosh rise to almost seven thousand feet elevation, and are among similar buttresses to the great mountain.

Right: Fish Lake and Cathedral Rock are in the Central Cascades northeast of Snoqualmie Pass. The lake is among several of the sources of the Cle Elum River.

Below: Winter's late afternoon light spreads across a ranch in the Klickitat Valley north of the Columbia River. Mount Adams, on the eastern Cascade edge, is in the distance, its summit obscured by clouds.

Right: Alpine fir cast long shadows on the snow on a winter's morning in Mount Rainier National Park. The sun, shining through the tip of the center tree, seems to create a corona as the light refracts in crystals of frost floating in the surrounding, freezing air.

Below: The huge Banks Lake Reservoir is a part of Central Washington's Columbia Basin Irrigation Project. At sunset, a flight of Canada geese migrate north as fishermen on the shore cast out their lines.

Right: Wheat. Heads, heavy with kernels, bend in the sunlight of Eastern Washington's wheat country.

Below: Icicles are uncommon in the Northwest's mild winters. Here, reflecting colored lights, they seem purposely chosen as decorations for winter holidays.

Right: Brilliantly colored vine maple leaves brighten Western Washington in autumn. Vine maple is not a *vine*, but is a small tree, or shrub, with slender and often curved or even contorted trunk and branches, and rarely exceeds fifteen feet in height. It is very common in all of the Douglas fir and hemlock forests.

Below: Sunset on Deception Pass lights the turbulent waters between Whidby and Fidalgo islands. The narrow channel is the principal tidal entrance-exit for a thirty-mile-long stretch of northern Puget Sound.

Right: Virgin forests of Douglas fir, spruce and hemlock cover many of the Olympic Mountains foothills in Northwest Washington's Olympic National Park.

Below: Sailboats on Lake Washington, in Seattle, maneuver for position for the start of an evening race. Distant horizon is the Cascade Mountain Range.

Right: Logs in booms await final processing near a mill in Port Angeles Harbor on Juan de Fuca Strait.

For assistance while preparing the text for "Washington," the writer gratefully acknowledges: Mrs. Hazel E. Mills, Washington State Library, Olympia, for reading, and for comments on, the general introduction and the regional introductions; Mr. Joseph R. Bianco, editor, *Northwest Magazine* of the Sunday *Oregonian* newspaper, Portland; persons in the Washington State Agencies at the State Capital, Olympia; persons in the U. S. Departments of Agriculture, Commerce and the Interior, Seattle; and to the personnel at the central, downtown Seattle Public library.

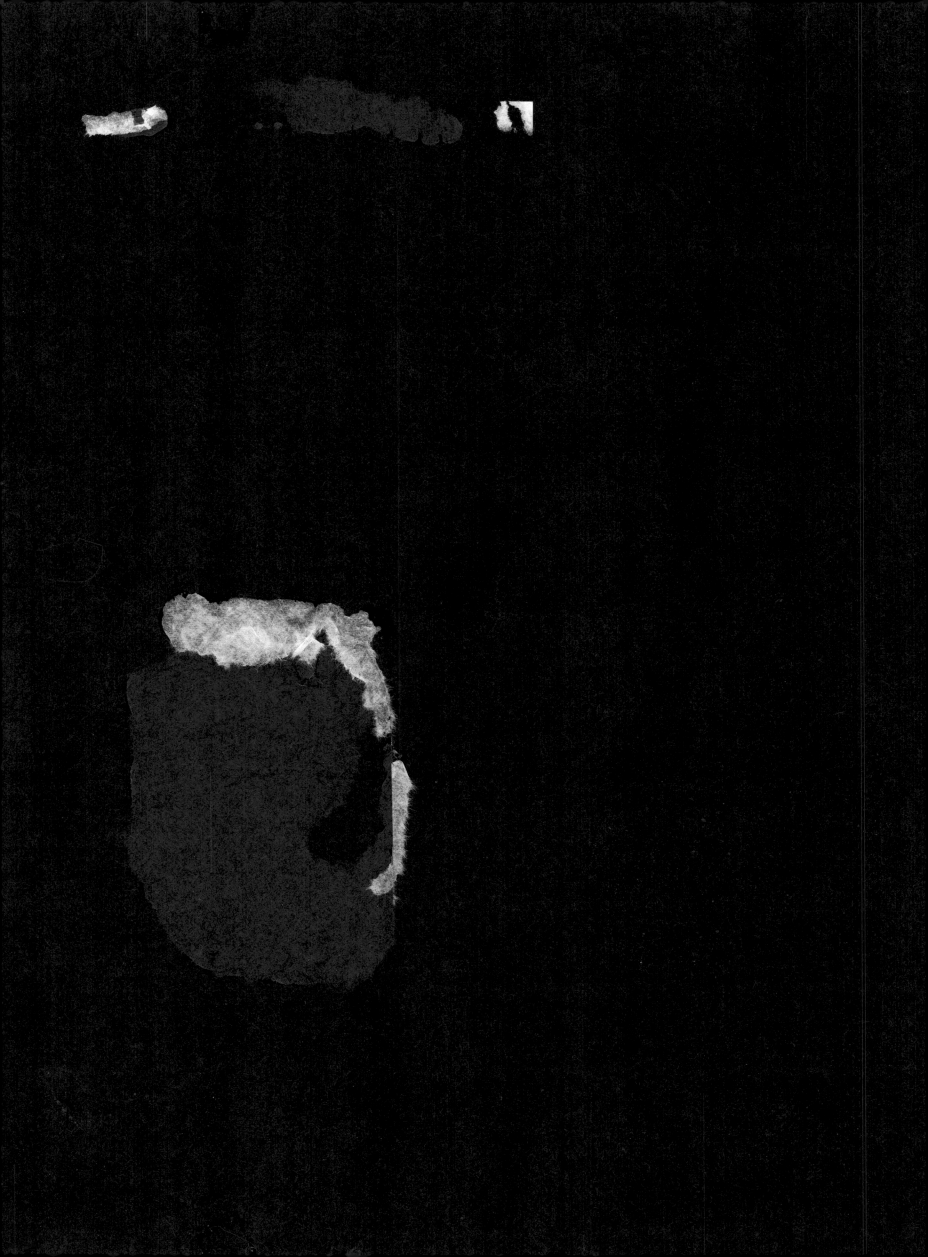